Truth Seekers Kids Magazine

January - 2023 | Issue 10

TS Kids Magazine Team

Mentor
Maulana Syed Abul Qasim Rizvi
& Syed H. Riza

Contributors
Jafar Hasan, Rabab,
Zahra Hasan, Smana Ali,
Insiya Fatima

Designer/Artwork
TS Kids Creative Team

Graphics/Images
TS Kids Creative Team
Mohd. Mehdi

For subscription, advertising, feedback and correspondence please contact:

magazine@tskids.club

TSKidsClub **TSKidsClub**

From the **Editor's Desk**

Dear Readers,

Salam-un alaykum,

Welcome to Issue 10 of TSKids Magazine. With all your love and support, what an amazing journey it has been - for this we thank you!

We start with business as usual - our Superhero, Lessons with Grandpa and Al-Kisa's Animals in the Quran series shedding light on important life lessons. In the Superhero series, Muhammad and Abdullah fight the thug. We have articles on Two Pieces of Bread, Ghadeer, and Hashim The Bread Breaker, as well as exciting poems, puzzles and more.

As you may be aware, we have recently launched the Truth Seekers Members Hub. Please look inside for details on how to become a member. We have also recently self-published some excellent picture-books for young readers including a series of 4 short books - Know Your Faith. They are freely available in soft copy if you are a TS Member and you may also buy them from our website.

We sincerely appreciate and rely on your continued support, generosity and prayers. We request your kind donations so that children can benefit from quality content and material.

Regards,

TS Editorial Team

The Helper

By Jafar Hasan

Take that

POW!

SMASH!

Let's go quickly. He will stay here for a while
Woah!

You are so strong. How did you do that?
It's nothing. Remember all power and courage comes from Allah alone. If you have conviction and a strong belief in Allah, then nobody can make you feel weak. Only Allah is al-Qawiyy (The Strong One). May Allah grant both of us strength to follow our religion and to not bow to anyone except Him.

So, where should I drop you?
Airport will do. Let me inform my parents.

Allah is Always There

By Zahra Hasan

When it gets dark in the night
And the world is sleeping tight

Our thoughts and our fear
There's no one to share

You might think you're alone
But you're never on your own

Allah is always there
Allah is everywhere

At the bottom of the sea
Or high up on the tree

Far out in the sky
With all the birds that fly

Amidst the stars that shine
And the galaxies, sublime

Allah is always there
Allah is everywhere

You may stand alone to pray
Many duas you may then say

Either said out aloud
Or whispered in your heart

Closer than the jugular vein
From no one is he ignorant

Allah is always there
Allah is everywhere

Lessons with Grandpa

Karbala, Love and Imam Hussain

By Syeda Rabab Zehra

Jamila was sitting beside the window, gazing at the colourful flowers in the garden. She was lost deep in her thoughts; 'but why did he get killed when he was the dearest to Allah? Allah has power over everything, then why did he leave him to be martyred?'. Her mind was full of questions that troubled her. Grandpa, who was clipping the plants in the garden, saw the puzzled face of Jamila and he could tell that something was bothering her. He took off his gardening gloves and came to the living room. "This time the roses grew bigger than before, didn't they?", he asked Jamila. Jamila was taken by surprise, "Oh, I didn't notice the roses Grandpa, sorry. I have been thinking about something else", she replied.

"What is it that troubles you my dear child?", Grandpa asked politely and sat next to Jamila. It was the month of Muharram, the month of commemoration of the martyrdom of Imam Hussain (peace be upon him). Jamila had been listening to the events that took place in Karbala and as usual, she pondered over what she listened to. "Grandpa, why did Allah not save Imam Hussain and his companions? They were following the path of truth and always obeyed Allah, so why were they so brutally killed?", Jamila asked. Grandpa looked at her and smiled as if he was pleased with Jamila's question. She had started to think deeply about realities in the lives of the imams.

Grandpa asked her "Is getting killed in the path of truth bad for a person?".

"Well, life is the most precious thing we have, isn't it Grandpa?", Jamila eagerly replied. "Besides that, it must have been so painful for them when they were hit with swords and for their family to witness their pain", she added, her eyes starting to fill with tears. Grandpa could see the confusion in Jamila's thoughts. On one hand, she knows that Allah is merciful to His creation and doesn't leave the pure ones alone, and on the other, she is sorrowful about the tragedy that took place in Karbala. Her mind couldn't reconcile the two things. This question was the same that troubled Grandpa in his youth, and he wanted to explain it to both his grandchildren, so he called Yusuf as well.

Yusuf had just finished his homework. He came and sat next to Grandpa on the couch. "Are you going to tell us a story, Grandpa?", Yusuf asked. "No, my son, not a story but a reality of life", Grandpa replied.

Grandpa faced Jamila and said, "Do you remember a few weeks ago when you went swimming while your arm was wounded?".

"Yes Grandpa, and it was even bleeding", Jamila replied.

"But did you notice the pain when you were swimming?" Grandpa asked.

"Swimming was so fun that I only noticed the wound while I was showering later", she chuckled.

"So, when your attention was completely on your swimming lesson, you didn't realise that your body was hurt?" Grandpa asked her.

"That's right Grandpa, and that's pretty amazing", Jamila said.

"Something similar once happened to me as well, Grandpa", Yusuf cried. "I was playing cricket and scratched my knee while trying to catch the ball. It hurt a bit, but I carried on until the end. When I was changing my uniform, I saw that my skin was peeled, and blood was caked on my knee. I was surprised that the wound was so deep, and I didn't even feel it!" Grandpa was making the two kids realise something important. He said, "So both of you have experienced that we need to pay attention to feel the pain in our body. If somebody pinched us while we were sleeping, we probably wouldn't notice it the same way as during our wakefulness, right?" Both kids nodded in affirmation.

"You see my lovely buds, we forget our pain when we are engrossed in something important or captivating to us. Imam Baqir (peace be upon him) was once asked about the intensity of pain that the martyrs of Karbala felt. Imam Baqir pinched the skin of his finger and said only this much."

"How is that possible?" Yusuf surprisingly asked. There was a moment of silence as Grandpa wanted the kids to think for themselves. After a while, Jamila spoke, "Imam Hussain was engrossed in fulfilling the commands of Allah and the wounds and injuries on his body didn't distract him even a bit", she said.

"Indeed, not only Imam Hussain but also his noble companions", Grandpa added.

"Now, to answer your other questions my dear daughter", Grandpa continued, "It is correct that the most precious thing we have is our life but does our life end with our body?"

"We live forever Grandpa, even after our body perishes", Yusuf exclaimed. Grandpa nodded and asked Jamila to bring the Holy Quran from the shelf. He opened the Quran and recited a verse from Surah Ale-Imran: "Do not consider those who are killed in our path as dead; they are alive and receive sustenance from us." Grandpa then went on to explain that those who are killed in the path of Allah experience life at its highest level, and as a reward Allah gives respect to their bodies as well. When they are buried in the ground, their bodies do not rot or stink, rather they remain fresh and fragrant.

"But then why do we cry over Imam Hussain in the mourning ceremonies, Grandpa?" Yusuf innocently asked.

"We cry for what people did to Imam Hussain and his family, not what came to him from Allah. Remember what Imam Hussain's sister Bibi Zainab (peace be upon her) said when the cruel Ibne Ziyad asked her "Zainab, did you see what Allah did to your brother?" She replied magnanimously: "I didn't witness anything but beauty." Meaning she saw beauty all along in what she and her family received from Allah. But when she gave her sermon in Kufa to people, she condemned them saying that they have committed a hideous sin and deserve to weep over their actions." The puzzled expressions on Jamila's face were starting to fade away.

Grandpa slightly bent towards Jamila and whispered in her ears "Can a person sacrifice everything for Allah without His help?" Jamila hugged Grandpa tightly while tears began to trickle from her eyes. She said "Today I came to realise that Karbala is not only a tragedy that took place in 61 Hijri, it is a manifestation of love, beauty and one of the greatest manifestations of Allah's help that comes to believers."

Grandpa thanked Allah in his heart for the guidance that the Almighty provided to him and his kids and hugged both his grandchildren.

From:

AL-KISA FOUNDATION
UNDER THE CLOAK OF GUIDANCE AND MERCY

Animals in the Quran

Prophet Ismail (A) & The Sheep

1

There once was a great Prophet of Allah, named Prophet Ibrāhīm ('a).* Prophet Ibrāhīm and his wife Hadrat Hājar* had a beautiful son named Ismā'īl ('a). He was also a prophet!
Prophet Ibrāhīm ('a) loved his son very much! He taught him all about Allah, and how Allah was the Most Wise and Most Powerful! He told his son that we should always trust Allah because He knows best. In turn, Ismā'īl ('a) began teaching others in Mecca about Allah, too!

2

One night, Prophet Ibrāhīm (●a) had a slightly scary dream.
In his dream, he saw himself sacrificing his dear son Ismā●īl (●a)!
Since he was a Prophet of Allah, he knew that his dream was a message from Allah. When he had the same dream the next night, and again the following night, he knew what he had to do.
He loved his son very much, but he loved Allah even more! He knew that Allah definitely had a good reason for this. After all, Allah is the Most Wise and He knows best!

3

4

The next day, Prophet Ibrāhīm ('a) said to Ismā'īl ('a), "My dear son, I keep having the same dream where I sacrifice you. What do you think we should do?"

Prophet Ismā'īl ('a) asked, "Dear Father, is this a command from Allah?"

Prophet Ibrāhīm ('a) answered, "Yes, this is a command from Allah, the Most Wise!"

Prophet Ismā'īl ('a) smiled and replied, "Then, we must do what Allah has ordered! Inshā'Allāh He will help me to be patient!"

5

6

The next day, both father and son began their journey to a far away land. On the way, Shay'ān* came up to them, pretending to be a man.
He asked, "Where are you taking your son, Ibrāhīm? Are you going to sacrifi ce him?! Are you sure you want to? How could you do this to your own son?!"
Both Prophet Ibrāhīm ('a) and Ismā'īl ('a) trusted Allah and knew Shay'ān was just trying to trick them. So, they decided to shoo him away! Prophet Ibrāhīm ('a) began throwing seven pebbles in his direction until he fi nally left them alone.

7

Then, they continued their journey with hearts full of faith! After a while, they finally reached their destination. Ismā'īl ('a) laid himself on a rock. Wow! He trusted Allah so much! Prophet Ibrāhīm ('a) closed his eyes, said Bismillāh, and began to perform the sacrifice.
All of a sudden, he heard a voice call out, "O Ibrāhīm! You have listened to and followed Allah's command! Now, sacrifice the sheep Allah has placed for you instead of Ismā'īl ('a)."

8

As Prophet Ibrāhīm ('a) slowly opened his eyes, he was shocked! There, on the very rock where Ismā'īl ('a) had just been, now lay a sheep! He looked around and saw a smiling Ismā'īl ('a) standing nearby, safe and alive! Sub'ānAllāh!

This was a really hard test for Prophet Ibrāhīm ('a), but he trusted Allah! In the end, he passed the test and made Allah happy! Allah sent His blessings on Prophet Ibrāhīm ('a), and young Ismā'īl ('a) returned home with his father unharmed.

9

10

Every year on Eid al-Adhā, Muslims all over the world sacrifice a sheep and give its meat to the poor and needy. By doing this, we remember the beautiful story of Prophet Ibrāhīm ('a) and how he always listened to Allah!

The story of Prophet Ibrāhīm ('a) and Prophet Ismā'īl ('a) teaches us to trust Allah. Allah is the Most Wise, and He knows what is best for us, even when we don't!

Match the Names

Nafi Bin Hilal	A tyrant governor of Kufa who ordered the killing of Imam Hussain (pbuh) on behalf of Yazid
Umar Ibne Sa'ad	A companion of Imam Ali (pbuh). He defended Imam Hussain (pbuh) on the day of Ashura using arrows with inscription on them
Wahab-e Kalbi	Reciter and teacher of Quran in the mosque of Kufa. He was so happy and eager for martyrdom that on the morning of Ashura he was making jokes with his companions.
Ubaidullah ibne Ziyad	Son of a companion of the Holy Prophet (pbuh). A commander in Karbala in charge of killing Imam Hussain (pbuh) in exchange for the rulership of Rey
Burrair-e Hamdani	Reverted to Islam from Christianity with his family and stayed with Imam Hussain (pbuh)

Two Pieces of Bread

By Insiya Fatima

Our pure, 12 imams during their noble lives were always keen to raise the living standards of poor people and guide them out of the difficult conditions they were in. Our imams helped them not only by giving them money or things, but in many other ways as well. While helping any person, the imams, who were sent as guides to humanity, would be involved in helping them become better people and better Muslims. All our imams worked very hard and made many sacrifices in carrying food and clothing on their shoulders to deliver them to the poor in the city, which was often done unknowingly. It was not the manners of the imams to display their charity and make the poor embarrassed in public. In the following story, we observe how Imam Sajjad (peace be upon him) helps a poor believer while also looking after his honour and guiding him and his family to the path of higher morals.

One day, a very poor man who was once rich came to the house of our fourth imam, Hazrat Ali bin Hussain (peace be upon him), and told the imam about his hardships and financial situation he was in. He said, "I was once a rich man but when I lost my work, I gradually lost everything. My financial condition keeps on getting worse and now I can't even provide food for my family." Then he sighed and asked the imam, "Can you help me?" Since the imam is a true representative of Allah on this earth, he knew that Allah does not like a believer to express his poverty before anyone else. Because of this reason, the imam at first did not encourage the person asking for help. Imam Sajjad replied, "I don't have anything now in the house that I can help you with but be patient and Allah shall grant you your necessity."

The man left the house of Imam Sajjad with a bit of shock and discouragement. When he stepped out of the door, he saw some people who didn't believe in Islam, sitting around and looking at him. They had seen the man eagerly going inside the house of Imam Sajjad and coming out with a serious expression, and hence they realised that he did not get what he went for. They then began mocking him by saying, "Didn't you believe your imam was capable of doing miracles? In that case, he could have easily fulfilled your wishes. What kind of religion is this whose leaders don't even care about the wellbeing of their followers?!" Hearing this, the man became upset and very angry. He furiously went back to the imam's house to express his anger and concern. When the imam heard him, he realised that this man's level of faith is not very high, so he said, "I only have two pieces of bread which I'm going to give you. But Allah is beneficent so be thankful and patient and he will grant you what you need." The man stepped outside and noticed that the bread was dry to the point that it wasn't going to make a proper dinner, but still, he thought, something is better than nothing. So, he put the two loaves of bread in his bag and moved along.

On the way home, he saw a fisherman who had low-quality fish, which was not very fresh. He asked the fisherman if he could trade the fish for one loaf of bread. The fisherman looked at the state the man was in - his clothes and their poor quality - so he agreed and gave him the fish. The fisherman thought to himself that after all, the fish would have spoiled in a day or two anyway. The poor man was now left with one loaf of bread and one low-quality fish. But he wanted something else to cook the fish with.

After a while the poor man saw a grocery store and decided to purchase some salt to make the fish more edible. So he went inside the store and said to the owner, "I have no salt in my house. Will you please be kind enough to accept this piece of bread for some salt?" The store owner also observed the poor man's outfit, felt mercy in his heart and accepted the offer. So now all the bread was gone and the fish with some salt remained.

Finally, he arrived home after a tough day and told his wife everything that happened. His wife did not lament or complain but instead replied believingly, "It's alright. Allah is Merciful and Beneficent. He will help us." Then she got busy cooking whatever her husband had brought home. They didn't know that there was a huge surprise waiting for them. As she started to cut the fish, she noticed that her knife was being blocked while slicing the fish, so she started to cut around the fish to see what it was inside. Sitting inside the fish lay a precious diamond. The poor man and family stared at it in shock and straight away they realized what Imam Sajjad meant by having patience. They learnt that Allah helps the believer from ways which are unthinkable to them.

Soon they heard a knock at the door. They stared at each other and were all thinking the same thing, "Could that be the fisherman coming to get his diamond back?" When they opened the door, it was the fisherman, but he only came to return the bread and said, " This bread is too dry. I cannot eat it, but you can have the fish too, I don't want it back." After a while the store owner knocked at the door with the same intentions as the fisherman and gave the loaf of bread he received back to the man. Now they had both loaves of bread as well. The diamond helped them to live more comfortably.

Activity:

Can you pick at least three morals we can learn from this story?

Word Search
Martyrs of Karbala

L U Y U S Y R J H A H J O T B

X G S J R N M A L A H X H U Y

G T U N K Z G I B Z B N S Z H

T A H F X D A M U K X I K P H

K M E G D S P H R W A N B B F

K W T K G F A L D Y R I I L U

A E R H A I B U R A I R L M N

H Z A X R H U A O E N W Y A S

M R V H S P B C W G F F C T Z

I L M M Y L D X C Z Q Z Y X E

S K J G X H S A B B A R S T G

A E O T H L Y R T D V Y Y J F

Q D H P T K R G V D Z I F Y H

H B N N J U Y P H G J S I U O

L A L I H N I B E F A N E I W

Abbas • Burair • John • Zuhair • Ali Akbar • Habib • Nafebin Hilal

Find the names of the martyrs of Karbala.
They can be in any direction, and they can share letters as they cross over each other.

Ghadeer-e-Khum

By Rabab

Towards the end of his life, our beloved Prophet Mohammad (peace be upon him) decided to perform the hajj to the Holy Kaaba. It was in the 10th year after the Prophet's migration to the city of Medina. This was the first and last Hajj of the life of our beloved prophet.

When the Holy Prophet announced that he was planning to go to hajj, a large number of Muslims packed their bags and requested the Prophet to let them accompany him.

Imam Ali (peace be upon him), the Prophet's successor, was not in the city of Madina where they lived; he had gone on a trade expedition to Yemen. The Holy Prophet, alongside the Muslims, reached the Holy city of Makkah on the 4th of Zilhajj. Imam Ali joined the Holy Prophet in Makkah and together they performed Hajj.

The profit that Imam Ali had earned in his expedition was also used for sacrificing animals in Hajj. Many animals were sacrificed whose meat was served to the Muslims during Hajj.

When all the rituals of Hajj finished and Muslims were returning to Madina, the Prophet received a revelation from Allah near a place known as Ghadeer-e-Khum. The arch angel Jibrael descended upon the Prophet and conveyed the message of Allah:

"O Esteemed Messenger, impart the guidance that has been revealed to you, and if you do not do it, it is as though you have not imparted His message at all". As soon as the Prophet received the revelation from Allah, he stopped the caravan and asked the muezzin Bilal to recite the Adhan.

The people who had gone ahead of the caravan were called back and those who were behind the caravan were waited for.

The Holy Prophet commanded people to untie the saddles of their camels. The saddles of all the camels were piled on top of one another to make a 'pulpit'.

Once all the people had gathered, the Prophet went up to the pulpit and asked Imam Ali to stand by his right. It was the season of summer and the Muslims were standing on the hot desert sand in love of Allah to listen to their beloved prophet.

The Prophet addressed the Muslims and said "All praise belongs to Allah. It is only Allah who I have my faith in and from Him do I seek all help." The Prophet at one point asked the Muslims, "Do you bear witness that there is no God but Allah and I am His servant and His prophet who is speaking to you right now, and do you believe that the Day of Judgment, heaven and hell and the life in the hereafter are all real and will definitely happen? The people replied, "Yes O Prophet, truly we believe."

The Prophet continued, "Allah has told me that I will soon be taken away from you, but I am leaving behind two heavy things: the book of Allah and my Ahlul bait. If you attach yourself closely to them you shall never be misguided. These two will never separate from one another until they meet me at the Pool of Kausar. Therefore, O people, it is my last will for you to remain close to the Quran and Ahlul bait until your death."

Then the Prophet asked who they think is worthier of obedience than their own selves. The people remained silent and didn't give any specific reply to the prophet. The Prophet then asked the people "Am I not worthier of obedience than you?" they answered immediately, "Yes truly you are."

Then Holy Prophet bent down and took the hand of Imam Ali in his blessed hands and said "Man kuntu Molahu fa haza Aliun mola" (whoever believes I am his master, this Ali is also a master to him).

After the Prophet made this announcement, people came one after the other and congratulated Imam Ali on this great blessing of Allah. First the men came forward and congratulated Imam Ali saying "Ya Ali, indeed you have been granted a very high position by Allah". The first person to congratulate Imam Ali was Omar. After all men had met the Imam and given him greetings, the women also one after the other swore allegiance to the Imam.

Therefore, the day of ghadeer is a special day of celebration for believers because Allah made Imam Ali our Imam and granted us with this great blessing.

Indeed, an Imam is a blessing greater than any other blessing of Allah because the Imam is our guide in this world and our intercessor in the Hereafter. He is like a sun that takes away all the darkness of the night.

May Allah make us the true followers of Imam Ali and help us to follow his footsteps.

SUBSCRIBE TO

Truth Seekers **Kids** Magazine

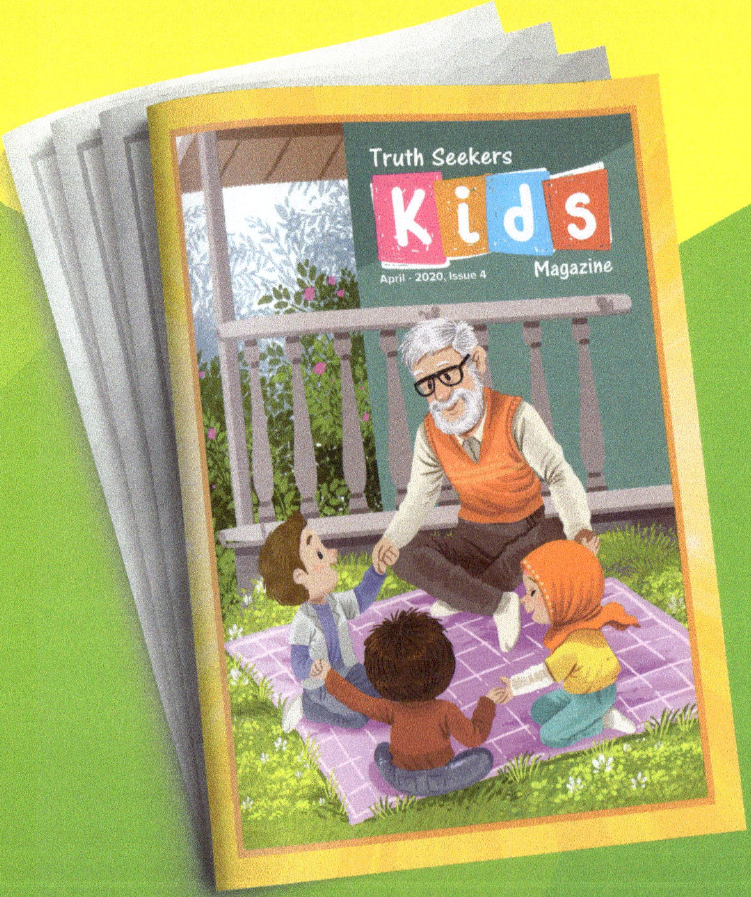

To subscribe, scan this QR Code:

$35 AU
Every year

TS Kids Magazine - Subscription of 4 issues & free shipping

TS Kids Magazine hard copy 4 issues delivered in Australia
Free shipping | Digital version available on request

For subscription in other countries
Please contact us at:
magazine@tskids.club
For more info, visit us at:
www.tskids.club/plans-pricing

Please Follow and Like our Instagram and Facebook pages to get updates about TS Kids Magazine and much more.

TSKidsClub   TSKidsClub

For more details, please visit **www.tskids.club/plans-pricing**

Little Contributors

By **Dimisha, grade 9**

By **Fatima Hasan, age 8**

By **Anaya Naqvi, age 8**

SUBMIT YOUR WORK

Hey kids! Would you like to submit your poem, writing or drawing?

Send it to us by email at **magazine@tskids.club**

Hashim The Bread Breaker

By Smana Ali

Artwork: Mohd. Mehdi (Age 14)

The Famine

The sun shone mercilessly on the land of Makkah. There had been no rain in a long time and the people were suffering from a famine. The food was short and many people went hungry, many times not knowing when their next meal would come.

Amr, the noble son of Abde Manaf could not bear to see the suffering of his people anymore. He was, like his ancestors, a believer in Tawheed (Oneness of God) who deeply cared for his people. He took all his wealth and made his way to Syria. After days of travelling, he reached Syria. He gave away all his wealth to buy food for his people. After returning to Makkah, every day he slaughtered his camels for gravy, and bread was broken to eat with the gravy. Everyone was then invited to eat from it.

This continued until the famine was over and all lives were saved.

The people of Makkah, touched by this act of generosity and kindness, named him Hashim, meaning the one who breaks bread. So he became popularly known as Hashim instead of his real name, Amr.

Bringing Hope

Although the famine was over, there was still a lot of poverty in Makkah. Sometimes when a poor family could not feed itself, they would go out in the desert and stay in a tent until death took all family members one by one. They would do this to protect their honour so that no one finds out about their miserable condition.

Hashim encouraged people to fight poverty and not give up. He suggested partnering one rich person with a poor one. The poor person would help the rich person in his trade and in return, the rich person would share his profit from the trades with the poor person. This way the poor families were able to earn an honourable livelihood themselves.

Efforts for Peace and Safety

There were yet many problems faced by the trade caravans of Makkah. Sometimes they were attacked and looted on their way while travelling in the desert. Other times, they were made to pay heavy taxes for selling in other lands. Hashim solved these problems wisely. He went and met the rulers and chiefs of these lands and made agreements with them on behalf of the people of Makkah. He asked for safety and fewer taxes and in return, the trade caravans of Makkah would bring to their land the goods that they needed and sell them at a fair price. This was a great achievement. The people of Makkah could safely trade to earn a living now.

It is for this achievement of Hashim that Allah refers to it as a great bounty of God upon Quraish in the holy Quran:

For the security and safeguard enjoyed by the Quraish, their safety during (their) journeys by winter and by summer, let them worship the Lord of this House who provides them with food against hunger, and with security against fear. (Qur'an, Ch. 106)

By now Hashim was considered the undisputed leader of the people of Makkah. They loved and obeyed him wholeheartedly.

Love for Allah and His house

Being a true believer in Tawheed, Hashim deeply cared for the Ka'aba and the people who came for Hajj pilgrimage. As soon as the moon of Zilhajjah was sighted, he walked to the Ka'aba with dignity and announced that all his wealth was available to feed and serve the pilgrims. He encouraged others to do the same.

The Jealous Nephew

As is obvious, the majority of the people of Makkah loved Hashim. However sadly, his very own nephew (the son of his twin brother Abdu Shams) was very jealous of his uncle. Ummaya would not let go of any opportunity to express his hatred for his uncle. He wanted to turn people's love and respect towards himself instead of his uncle. Sometimes he would try to achieve this by giving people expensive gifts, but to no avail. He wanted the leadership of the people of Makkah for himself.

The fire of jealousy continued to burn in the heart of Umayyah. At last, he insisted upon his uncle that both of them should go to one of the sages (fortune-tellers) of Arabia and only he whom the sage considered to be wiser would be the leader of Makkah. Hashim did not want to argue or dispute with his nephew. When Ummaya insisted, Hashim agreed to go to the sage on two conditions: whoever would lose was to sacrifice 100 camels for the pilgrims and would remain out of Makkah for 10 years.

Finally, the day arrived for both Hashim and Umayya to go to the sage. As soon as the sage saw Hashim, he started to praise him and decided in his favour. Therefore, Umayya had to sacrifice 100 camels and he remained in Syria (outside Makkah) for 10 years.

Unfortunately, these 10 years in exile only increased the vengeance in his heart that fell on the children of Hashim in the years to come.

Hashim was very handsome, and because of his looks and prestige, many chiefs and even rulers wanted him to marry their daughters. But he married Salma, a virtuous lady living in Yathrib. She gave birth to a son, who was named Sheeba.

One day Salma was busy looking after their infant in her hometown of Yathrib when a man on horseback arrived at their house and knocked on the door in a panic.

She opened the door only to receive the sad news of the demise of her husband Hashim at the young age of 25 while he was in Ghazzah (Palestine).

It fills one with wonder, how someone can make so many achievements in such a short lifespan. Hashim's grave is still preserved in Ghazzah.

MASJID-E-HASHIM IN GHAZZAH IN WHICH HAZRAT HASHIM IS BURIED.

www.ingramcontent.com/pod-product-compliance
Ingram Content Group UK Ltd.
Pitfield, Milton Keynes, MK11 3LW, UK
UKHW062002290726
14090UKWH00021B/1344

9 780645 209112